RAF AIRCRAFT OF THE COLD WAR

AIR-TO-AIR IMAGES

TONY PAXTON

Key
Books

TITLE PAGE IMAGE: A Tornado F3 sets off a shockwave as it exceeds Mach 1.

CONTENTS PAGE IMAGE: 25 Squadron sported a 75th anniversary scheme on this Tornado F3.

COVER IMAGE: An F4 Phantom of 111 Squadron (Tremblers). Phantoms replaced the Lightnings when the squadron relocated to RAF Leuchars in Scotland.

BACK COVER IMAGE: 29 Squadron was the first Tornado F3 squadron. Here, the author flies in the back seat of one 29 Squadron aircraft whilst another fully armed aeroplane closes in for a photograph.

Published by Key Books
An imprint of Key Publishing Ltd
PO Box 100
Stamford
Lincs
PE19 1XQ

www.keypublishing.com

The right of Tony Paxton to be identified as the author of this book has been asserted in accordance with the Copyright, Designs and Patents Act 1988 Sections 77 and 78.

Copyright © Tony Paxton, 2020

ISBN 978 1 913295 84 4

20 21 22 23 24   10 9 8 7 6 5 4 3 2 1

Typeset by SJmagic DESIGN SERVICES, India.

CONTENTS

FOREWORD

The period of history known as the Cold War (1948 to 1991) was important for the development of air warfare. At the end of the Second World War, the Allies – the US, UK and USSR – were more shocked than they were prepared to reveal to each other at just how far ahead the Germans were with the development of jets, aeronautics, guided weapons and rockets. The formation of NATO in 1949 in response to the creeping advance of Soviet-friendly (later to be subjugated) communist regimes in Eastern Europe, relied on air power from the start to provide rapid response, air defence and conventional and nuclear deterrence.

This book, written and beautifully illustrated by an experienced Royal Air Force fast jet pilot, reminds us all of the vital role played by the Royal Air Force during that time. The fact is that some aeroplanes were better than others. For example, the author's passion for the English Electric Lightning is very clear. The aeroplane was built to react quickly, via quick reaction alert, and climb rapidly to intercept Soviet bombers with the first generation of air-to-air missiles. Other aircraft, such as the British Hunter and Canberra, were adapted to undertake a wide range of NATO missions. Tactics evolved to meet the perceived threat. For much of the Cold War, the Royal Air Force in Germany and the UK honed their skills at flying at very low level. The Tornado, procured with Germany and Italy, represents the acme of this art. Range was extended by air-to-air refuelling, and training and exercises were taken very seriously and assessed by NATO. Air forces were organised into Allied Tactical Air Forces with the RAF integrated into TWOATAF commanded by a British Air Marshal. For those involved, the Cold War was real in terms of posture and readiness. Squadrons worked and played hard.

Tony Paxton, an exceptional pilot, rarely without his camera, has created a record of this, too often overlooked, element of Royal Air Force history. I commend this book as an excellent addition to the canon of work on the time known as the Cold War.

Air Chief Marshal Sir Stuart Peach GBE, KCB, DL
Chairman NATO Military Committee and
RAF Canberra and Tornado Navigator

OPPOSITE: A Tornado F3 with the wings in the 67, fully swept position.

CHAPTER 1
A SHORT, EXPLANATORY HISTORY

The Cold War started in the aftermath of the Second World War. The victors divided the spoils amongst themselves by creating occupied sectors of Germany, and the Soviet Union took control of the area to the east, which became the German Democratic Republic, more commonly known as East Germany. Berlin, positioned in East Germany, was also split between the winning parties. Those countries invaded by Germany during the war fared differently depending upon which victorious ally was in control. The Western European countries returned to political normality and started to rebuild their infrastructure and economies. Those countries that bordered the new East Germany and the ones further to the East, up to the Russian border, came under Soviet jurisdiction. In 1948, the Soviet Union flexed its muscles and denied the western allies any access to Berlin via the road and rail links through East German territory. The intention was that the Western powers would walk away and leave the whole of Berlin to the Soviets. However, that was not to be, and the Western allies organised an airborne supply chain. There were three air corridors from West Germany into Berlin and a constant stream of transport aeroplanes ferried essentials into the besieged city. There was not only food but also fuel, both coal and petrol. At the height of the blockade, in April 1949, there was an aeroplane landing every minute. There were three airfields in use and even large flying boats were landing on Lake Havel. This extraordinary effort by the Western allies was to become known as the Berlin Airlift and lasted from June 1948 until late 1949, continuing for several months after the Soviets lifted their blockade in May 1949.

Prompted by the Soviet attitude and the spread of communism, the North Atlantic Treaty Organisation (NATO) was set up in 1949. It initially consisted of 12 North American and European countries and followed the premise that an attack on one was an attack on all.

OPPOSITE: The BAe Hawk started to replace the Folland Gnat as the RAF's advanced trainer in the late 1970s. This T Mk1 was with 4FTS based at RAF Valley but sported a CFS crest on the fin.

A PanAm Boeing 727 takes off from Templehof airport in the heart of Berlin. The 'Wall' can be seen in the background along the airport perimeter. PanAm had a US government contract to keep an air link between West Germany and Berlin. Templehof was used extensively during the Berlin Airlift.

In 1955, West Germany joined the alliance after being allowed to re-arm. It was probably this action that prompted the Soviet Union to set up the Warsaw Treaty Organisation, which became known as the Warsaw Pact, in May 1955. The Warsaw Pact had eight countries in its membership and where they bordered NATO and neutral countries there were heavily defended fences or walls and other defences, including minefields. This was as much to keep their own citizens in as to keep NATO forces out. The barrier stretched for over 4,000 miles and became known as the Iron Curtain, in reference to a speech made by Winston Churchill in 1946.

These two military organisations faced off against each other for the next 35 years, each ready to respond to an attack on any of its members. There were tensions and posturing on both sides, but no such attack ever happened, and this unsettled peace was what came to be known as the Cold War. It finally came to an end in 1991, following the dismantling of the Berlin wall and the overthrow of communist governments throughout Eastern Europe.

OPPOSITE: The Jet Provost was the basic trainer of the RAF throughout the 70s and early 80s. This is a T Mk4 from 3FTS at RAF Leeming.

The Berlin Wall was a continuation of the IGB within the city of Berlin. It was erected behind the façade of houses that were demolished to build it and a former road between the sectors was summarily blocked. On the Eastern side of the wall there were sterile strips of land, minefields and watch towers set within the perimeter fence.

CHAPTER 2
1970s CAMOUFLAGE AND DISPERSAL

By 1970, whilst very much alive and kicking, the Cold War had faded in the consciousness of most of the British public. The Berlin Airlift had been over 20 years earlier and the Cuban missile crisis was a distant memory. The four-minute warning, which was all the time that the British would have to take shelter, was supposedly a thing of the past, and the United Kingdom's nuclear deterrent had disappeared beneath the waves. In addition, the 'hot' war in Vietnam was a more tangible example of the dangers facing the Western world. The most public reminder of the ongoing Cold War was the emergence of various protest groups that had followed in the wake of CND.

The peace between the major powers was predominantly because of fear. The atomic bombs that were dropped on Hiroshima and Nagasaki were actually quite small weapons with a yield of only 20 kilotons. However, because of the construction of Japanese cities, where most of the buildings were made of wood and paper, the devastation was out of all proportion to the size of the bombs. Had those attacks been made on a typical European city, it is highly likely that most buildings would have remained standing, and the death toll would have been much smaller.

The nuclear weapons available by the 1970s were of the megaton variety, making them up to 25,000 times more powerful than those dropped by the USAAF in August 1945. Consequently, the concept of Mutually Assured Destruction (MAD) ensured that any attack would require extreme provocation or complete disregard for the effects of a retaliatory strike. A country's possession of high-yield nuclear warheads, whether on bombs or missiles, was an effective deterrent to any nation wishing to launch an attack.

Despite the apparent apathy of most of the British public, Britain's armed forces were only too well aware of the threat and there was continuous and intense training to counter it. In particular, the Royal Air Force had a range of aircraft and weaponry to both defend against, and respond to, an attack. As a result of wars and skirmishes in other parts of the world, the RAF was continually devising and evolving new practices. The Arab Israeli war of 1967, known as the six-day war, showed the vulnerability of bright aircraft neatly lined up on an aerodrome. Whole squadrons of Arab fighter aeroplanes were wiped out before they could even get airborne. A dozen natural metal-finish aircraft, neatly lined up next to each other in the open, were an easy target for the Israeli attack aircraft. These attacks ensured that Israel had air supremacy and were responsible for the very brief nature of the confrontation.

Throughout NATO there was a programme of dispersion and protection. Hardened Aircraft Shelters (HASs) were constructed in remote sites around fast jet airfields. These shelters would provide blast protection from any nuclear attack and their dispersed locations also made a successful conventional low-level attack, with guns or laydown weapons, less likely. Those aerodromes closest to the threat were equipped first, and by 1980 the RAF airfields of Bruggen, Wildenrath and Laarbruch in Germany had all their squadrons dispersed around the airfield; each with its own HAS site with supporting hardened operations

OPPOSITE: A Harrier GR3.

Lightnings lined up on the pan in Malta. An inviting target for any ground-attack aircraft.

Another tempting ground-attack target. F4s of 43 Squadron on the APC line at RAF Akrotiri in Cyprus.

blocks called Pilot Briefing Facilities (PBF). Later, with the disappearance of single-seat aircraft from the front line, they would become Crew Briefing Facilities (CBFs). RAF Gutersloh also had a degree of dispersal and protective capability in the form of revetments dispersed around the Southern side of the airfield. The revetments were circular pans surrounded by a high, earth and stone bank to provide blast protection from all but a direct hit. By 1980, Gutersloh was a Harrier base and, because their role was close air support of allied ground forces, the plan was for the aeroplanes to be dispersed forward, off base. This was made possible by their short take off and vertical landing capability. Gutersloh was the last RAF airfield in Germany to be fully hardened with HASs and CBFs.

The mainstay of the UK's air defence in the early 1970s was the English Electric Lightning and there were squadrons based in the UK, Germany,

A typical HAS site on a UK airfield.

A second generation HAS at RAF Bruggen in Germany. It has multi-angles to the roof and retains the recessed doors. The shelter has been built on the edge of one of the original revetments. This 31 Squadron GR1 is carrying two JP233 training rounds.

A final version of a HAS for the UK. Notice the sliding blast doors allowing maximum space inside, which is sufficient for two aircraft.

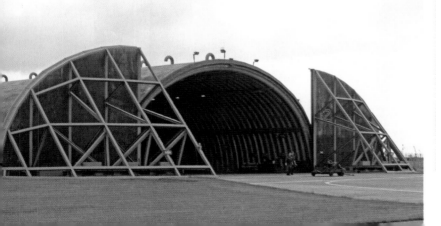

A side view of a UK HAS showing the jet blast deflector vents at the rear.

Cyprus, and Singapore. All of these aeroplanes had a natural metal finish; most of them with bright and colourful squadron markings, which made them highly visible to any attacking fighter bombers. Other front-line fast jets such as the RAF's new Harriers, the F4 Phantoms and the Buccaneers, had been delivered with a standard, grey/green camouflage paint scheme. Even the V-force Vulcans and Victors had had their ant-flash, white colour schemes replaced with the grey/green pattern following the change in role. No 74 Squadron, based at RAF Tengah, Singapore, disbanded in August 1971 and their Lightning F Mk6s were ferried to RAF Akrotiri in Cyprus, where they re-equipped No 56 Squadron which, up until then, had operated the shorter-range Lightning F Mk3. In January 1975, 56 Squadron was redeployed back to Wattisham in the UK. The first Lightnings to lose their all-metal finish were those based at RAF Gutersloh in Germany. Nos 19 and 92 squadrons had their aircraft topsides painted in an olive drab green, retaining the natural metal

This Victor K2 is a converted B2 and the grey/green camouflage replaced the original anti-flash white.

The Vulcans also received the new camouflage paint scheme.

finish below. In the UK, the threat of a low-level attack on Lightnings on the ground was not perceived to be as great as it was in Germany. For that reason, it would be some time before a camouflage scheme was applied. In fact, the Lightning squadrons at Wattisham, Nos 29 and 56, and No 23 at Leuchars in Scotland, had all re-equipped with the F4 Phantom before the Lightnings could be painted. RAF Binbrook in Lincolnshire became the RAF's only Lightning base and it was there that the aircraft acquired a grey/green camouflage scheme. In the mid-1980s, some aircraft were repainted with an overall grey finish.

OPPOSITE: A Tornado GR1 of 9 Squadron taxis from a HAS at RAF Honington in Suffolk.

43 Squadron was the first RAF air-defence Phantom squadron and was based at Leuchars.

A Tornado GR1 of 31 Squadron in a HAS at RAF Bruggen in Germany. Note the angular shape of the roof and that one of the two doors covering the blast vents at the rear is open.

A Lightning F Mk3 of 5 Squadron in natural metal finish.

This F Mk6 Lightning, on detachment to RAF Luqa for APC, is in all-metal finish and sports a Maltese Cross on the fin.

The UK Lightnings were painted in a conventional grey/green pattern in the 1970s. This 5 Squadron one is over a foggy Yorkshire coast near Flamborough Head.

The first Lightnings to be painted were the F Mk2As at RAF Gutersloh. This aeroplane was assigned to the author during his time in XIX Squadron. Note his name stencilled below the cockpit.

228 Operational Conversion Unit (OCU) trained crews for the RAF's Phantoms. This aeroplane is sporting a new overall grey colour scheme.

CHAPTER 3
AIR DEFENCE OF THE INNER GERMAN BORDER

The RAF's contribution to the airborne air defence of West Germany was two squadrons of Lightnings at RAF Gutersloh, some 80 miles from the border with East Germany. There were two aircraft holding a five-minute readiness state in a small hangar near the end of runway 27. The aeroplanes were fully armed with two Firestreak missiles and two 30mm Aden cannons. In an attached building were two pilots and six ground crew ready to respond to any alert that might be called. This facility, and the operation in general, was called Battle Flight. To prevent inadvertent infringements of East German airspace, and give an opportunity to identify any transgressors, there were two zones within NATO airspace abutting the border with the East. Immediately next to the Inner German Border (IGB) was the Air Defence Identification Zone (ADIZ), and against that was the Buffer Zone. Only traffic under the control of one of the German Air Force GCI (ground control intercept) radar stations was allowed into either of those zones. A legacy of the Berlin Airlift was the three air corridors that penetrated the Buffer Zone and ADIZ to provide air access to the divided city. Every year, RAF Gutersloh hosted aircraft from the US and French air forces for an exercise to demonstrate NATO's willingness to maintain the integrity of those air corridors. Over several days, transport aircraft from each nation would be escorted by fighters up and down an imaginary air corridor that paralleled the IGB and was close enough for all the activity to be visible to East German radars. The message was clear; we are willing to repeat the Berlin Airlift if necessary.

There were frequent scrambles of the Lightnings on Battle Flight. Being airborne in a supersonic fighter within five minutes was no mean feat, especially from a state of deep sleep. For this reason, the pilots slept fully dressed; some maybe removing their flying boots. A no-notice scramble would begin with a loud and very shrill bell triggered from the operations centre. The pilots and ground crew would rush straight to their allocated aircraft. The pilot's lifejacket would be hanging on the missile and donned as he climbed the ladder, his flying helmet would already be plugged into the oxygen system and the R/T lead. After settling into the seat, contact was made with operations, or the GCI station, via a secure link called telebrief. The check-in would be followed by information from operations or the GCI station and the instruction to standby. More often than not, it would be an immediate scramble, and the order would be something like: 'alert one, vector 090, climb angels 30, contact Crabtree on channel 12, SCRAMBLE, SCRAMBLE, SCRAMBLE'. All this time, the pilot would be completing his strap-in procedure and the ground crew would remove the ejection seat safety pins and the ladder. As soon as the first syllable of 'scramble' was uttered, the start button for the No 1 engine would be pressed; by the time the order was complete both engines would be running and the aeroplane starting to move. Air traffic control would have heard all of the communication, cleared any other traffic from the

OPPOSITE: 19 Squadron re-equipped with the F4 Phantom II. This aeroplane is fully armed with four Skyflash semi-active missiles, four Sidewinder heat-seeking missiles and a Vulcan (Gatling) 20mm cannon.

A 19(F) Squadron Lightning from Battle Flight at RAF Gutersloh scrambles.

area and as the Lightning approached the runway, immediate take-off clearance would be granted. Very often, the Battle Flight aircraft would be airborne in well under four minutes from the sounding of the initial alert bell. Most of these scrambles were for border patrols. The aeroplane would be cleared through the Buffer Zone and into the ADIZ to set up a North–South orientated racetrack pattern. There would always be a Warsaw Pact fighter flying a corresponding racetrack on the Eastern side of the IGB. At the time, the Lightning pilot would not know if he had been scrambled because of the eastern bloc aircraft, or vice versa. Occasionally, the scramble would be for a west-bound border crossing; these would generally be light aeroplanes smuggling goods or people across. Very rarely were they intercepted as they had landed somewhere and were concealed by the time that the Battle Flight fighter had reached the area. There were also infringements of the ADIZ. Once intercepted, the culprit would be escorted away from the border and shepherded to a landing somewhere the pilot could be questioned and subsequently face the wrath of the authorities.

In the event of hostilities, NATO's fighters would have manned a continuous series of combat air patrols (CAPs), from the Baltic coast all the way down to the Austrian border, (Austria being a neutral country). Gutersloh's Lightnings, and later F4s based at Wildenrath, would fly on patrols at high or low level. These search patterns were called a HLSP or LLSP and they had the support of the German Air Force ground intercept radars. In addition, if required, Victor tanker aircraft could be made available.

ABOVE AND OPPOSITE: The fighters involved with escorting transports in the *Field Fox* exercise corridor. Lightnings from 19 and 92 squadrons at Gutersloh, a USAF F4 Phantom from Bitburg and a French Mirage 3.

Exercise *Field Fox* hosted by RAF Gutersloh. Two USAF F4s take off with a French Air Force Transall about to taxi. A 19 Squadron pilot prepares to start engines so that he can join the F4s.

OPPOSITE: Lightning F2A of 19 Squadron refuels from a Victor K1. The F2A Lightning retained the top-mounted, integral Aden cannons and so the whole ventral tank was available for fuel.

A 19 Squadron F4 flies by a German Air Force radar intercept site.

OPPOSITE: A Lightning F2A of 19 Squadron on a low-level CAP near to the Eder Dam, one of the dams breached by 617 Squadron in May 1943.

CHAPTER 4
DEFENCE OF THE REALM AND THE FLEET

In the mid-1960s, the Labour government had committed to withdrawal from East of Suez, and the demise of the Royal Navy's fixed-wing capability. Therefore, in the 1970s, the RAF was tasked, not only with the defence of the UK mainland, but also defence of the fleet. The Royal Navy had three fixed-wing aircraft carriers. HMS *Hermes* was converted to helicopter operations and became a Royal Marine assault ship. (*Hermes* was later to return to fixed-wing operations with Sea Harriers and, during the Falklands conflict, RAF Harriers on board.) The remaining conventional fixed-wing ships were HMS *Eagle*, which was decommissioned in January 1972, and HMS *Ark Royal* which soldiered on until February 1979. Following her de-commissioning, *Ark Royal's* Phantoms and Buccaneers were transferred to the RAF.

The air defence of the realm was concentrated on the east coast of the UK, ready for any threat crossing the North Sea. There was a chain of land-based radar stations stretching from Saxa Vord, situated on the island of Unst, North Shetland, down to Neatishead in Norfolk. These air-defence radars were located on relatively high ground, close to the coast, so as to increase their range of detection for low-flying targets. Due to the geographical location of the British Isles, early warning was also

RIGHT: The air defence radar array on HMS *Kent*, a County-class destroyer armed with anti-aircraft missiles and a gun. This ship was intended primarily to defend aircraft carriers.

OPPOSITE: A glimpse of things to come. A Tornado F3 escorts a Boeing E3 Sentry from the NATO squadron at Geilenkirchen in Germany. Sentrys were bought by the MoD to replace the Shackletons and the ill-fated Nimrod AEW 3.

F4 Phantoms from the Leuchars wing. A 43 Squadron aeroplane formates on one from 111 Squadron.

ABOVE AND ABOVE RIGHT: A Russian Bear D intercepted by the author in the Iceland/Faroes gap in February 1976.

provided by NATO countries farther to the east. The most notable of these was Norway, which would make early radar contact with any Soviet aircraft transiting around North Cape to enter the North Sea, or heading towards the Iceland Faeroes gap, en route to Cuba or the Atlantic.

The airspace around the UK was, and still is, frequently traversed by Soviet military aircraft. To monitor such flights, but primarily to respond to any attack upon the UK, fully armed fighters were kept on constant readiness at bases on the east coast. Air defence QRA (Quick Reaction Alert), was divided into North and South. Northern QRA was held at RAF Leuchars near St Andrews in Fife. Southern QRA was shared between two bases, RAF Binbrook in Lincolnshire and RAF Wattisham in Suffolk. As in Germany, two aeroplanes were kept on standby in a hangar (or Q shed), near to the end of the runway. However, unlike

Battle Flight's five minutes, these aircraft and crews maintained a ten-minute readiness. This is because the North Sea and NATO allies to the east provided a reasonable degree of warning. The interloping aircraft were, in the 70s and 80s, predominantly Tupolev TU95 bomber and reconnaissance aircraft, NATO code name 'Bear', or Tupolev TU16s, code name 'Badger'. Occasionally, an Ilyushin IL20 reconnaissance and electronic intelligence (ELINT) aeroplane, code named 'Coot', would support Russian naval exercises or spy on NATO naval exercises in the waters around the UK.

The air defence of the UK was shared between two types of RAF fighter, the Lightning and the F4 Phantom, until 1987, when the Tornado ADV entered service. The Lightning had a superb rate of climb and was very fast. However, it was limited by its relatively poor radar,

A 23 Squadron Tornado F3 flies by the GCI station at Staxton Wold near Flamborough Head in Yorkshire.

OPPOSITE: Two Lightnings from 5 Squadron climbing steeply.

with virtually no look down capability, a small weapon load and limited range without AAR. The F4 had a very good radar, carried eight missiles and had a range that far surpassed that of the Lightning. However, Britain's F4s were highly modified from the original US fighter. They were mostly intended as ground-attack, or strike aircraft and, therefore, needed to be efficient during low-level flight. The UK's Buccaneer S2s, with a similar low-level role, were fitted with Rolls Royce Spey engines and that engine was also chosen to power the RAF's Phantoms. The Spey power plant was a low bypass turbofan and very efficient below 20,000ft and at subsonic speeds. However, it was bulkier than the General Electric J79 (which was very similar to the Lightning's Rolls Royce Avon turbojets) used in the USAF's F4s, and so gave the RAF's Phantoms a wider fuselage and a greater cross section, slightly increasing drag. The use of Spey engines significantly reduced their high-level performance and hindered their effectiveness at 40,000ft and above.

Due to the added requirement to provide air defence for the Royal Navy, a number of exercises were conducted in the Western Approaches, as well as the North Sea. Defence of the fleet needed a high degree of coordination between different assets, both navy and air force. The

Royal Navy had dedicated air-defence warships equipped with a capable air-detection radar and surface-to-air missiles (SAMs). There were very competent fighter controllers (known in the navy as Direction Officers) on board, and they were most efficient at controlling fighters onto any hostile targets. However, the radar range of a surface vessel was severely limited by the curvature of the Earth, and so there was continuous co-ordination with airborne early warning (AEW) assets. When the Royal Navy had had fixed wing carriers, AEW had been provided by Fairey Gannet aircraft equipped with an old AN/APS20 radar from the 1950s. To provide the RAF with an AEW capacity, the Gannets' radars had been fitted to Avro Shackleton Mk2 aeroplanes. The Shackleton had been a mainstay of the RAF's maritime surveillance and anti-submarine warfare capability for decades, until it was replaced by the Nimrod. The most modern version was the Mk3 with a nose-wheel, tricycle configured undercarriage. However, that airframe did not provide sufficient ground clearance to fit the required radar scanner and so the tail-wheel equipped Mk2 was chosen. During the late 1970s, there was a project to replace the AEW Shackleton with a version of the Nimrod, which was nicknamed 'Nimwacs'. However, it proved to be a bit of a disaster and was dropped in favour of acquiring the AWACS (airborne warning and control system). AWACS was a highly modified Boeing 707 with a large radome containing a rotating scanner mounted above the central fuselage; in UK service it was named 'Sentry'. The RAF's Nimrod maritime surveillance aircraft provided an anti-submarine shield as well as a search-and-rescue service for fighters operating far from land. The most important support for the fighters

An F4 Phantom from 111 Squadron displays its load of 4 Skyflash and 4 Sidewinder missiles.

was, of course, the tanker force. Victors, VC10s and Tristars allowed the Lightnings, Phantoms, and later the Tornado F3s, to spend much longer on task and farther from land than would otherwise be possible. RAF Vulcans were modified for use in a maritime radar surveillance role. They would locate unidentified surface vessels which would then be identified and, if necessary, attacked by RAF Buccaneers using Martell anti-ship missiles.

ABOVE AND OVERLEAF: An AEW Shackleton of 8 Squadron with the bulge under the forward fuselage housing the radar scanner.

A 111 Squadron F4 flies by the Forth bridges.

Norwegian air force F16s hand over to an RAF QRA aeroplane.

OPPOSITE: RAF Buccaneers of 12 Squadron fly by a bridge across the river Meuse as it flows through Maastricht.

A Lightning F6 of 11 Squadron, accompanied by an F3 from 5 Squadron, coasts out over Cleethorpes having departed from RAF Binbrook.

The first Tornado ADV squadron was 29 Squadron based at RAF Coningsby.

Buccaneer S2s of 12 Squadron in transit.

OPPOSITE: Nimrod AEW 3 was a project that never came to fruition because of problems with the computer systems and cost overruns. It was cancelled in 1986 in favour of the Boeing E3 Sentry.

A Nimrod MR1 of 203 Squadron lands at RAF Luqa on Malta in the early 1970s.

A Nimrod MR2 descends toward base.

Two Lightnings refuel from a Victor K2 of 57 Squadron.

OPPOSITE: A VC10 tanker of 101 Squadron with two Tornado 'chicks' in tow.

A Tornado F3 takes fuel from a 216 Squadron Tristar's centreline hose.

Mixed Fighter Force (MFF) was a way of increasing the weapon load of a Tornado F3. This Hawk has a gun fitted but for the real thing would have had two AIM9 infrared missiles and would follow directions from the Tornado navigator.

CHAPTER 5
AIR-TO-AIR REFUELLING, THE FORCE MULTIPLIER

Tanker aircraft are used by the RAF for two main reasons. Firstly, the use of air-to-air refuelling (AAR) allows relatively short-range aeroplanes to transit long distances without having to stage through airports to refuel. This allows rapid deployment to areas of tension or for the reinforcement of units under threat. Secondly, in-flight refuelling also supports UK air defence fighters by permitting them to remain on task for extended periods. This tactic means that four fighters can remain on CAP for many hours instead of eight fighters having to rotate through their base to refuel. When QRA is scrambled, AAR also allows the intercept to occur further from UK shores than would otherwise have been possible.

RAF aircraft use the probe and drogue method of air-to-air refuelling. The tanker trails a hose with a basket-shaped drogue at the end. The hose is approximately 70ft long. The pilot of the receiving aeroplane manoeuvres behind the tanker and positions its probe behind the drogue. Power is then applied so as to advance and make contact. A further application of power winds the hose onto a drum as the fighter moves forward and several rotations of the drum opens a valve that allows fuel to flow into the receiver's tanks. Victor and VC10 tankers had three refuelling points. There was a pod under each wing for fast jets, which permitted two aeroplanes to refuel at the same time. Mounted on

OPPOSITE: Harriers, including a trainer version, of 4 Squadron top up from a 55 Squadron Victor.

A VC10 transport of 10 Squadron refuelling from a VC10 tanker of 101 Squadron.

A Tornado F3's pilot view of the approach to the centreline hose of a Tristar.

In contact with the Tristar 'fuel flows'.

Two Jaguars of 6 Squadron with a Victor.

the centre line, at the rear of the fuselage, was a larger hose drum unit with a slightly bigger drogue. Although this centre line hose could be used by all types, it was primarily used by large receivers. They might be maritime surveillance aircraft, large bombers, transports or other tankers. The Victor K2 tanker was unable to take off with a full fuel load. However, it was quite capable of flying whilst full. For this reason, if a deployment of fast jets was underway, two Victors would take off and, once at top of climb, one would fully refuel the other before returning to base. Using such a procedure, one Victor K2 could take 4 fighters from the UK to Cyprus.

OPPOSITE: A Tornado GR1 navigator's view of contact with a Victor.

The 'boomer's' position at the rear of a KC135.

The view from over the shoulder of the 'boomer'.

The USAF uses a completely different method to transfer fuel from tanker to receiver. Taking the KC135 (from which the Boeing 707 was derived) as an example, the aircraft has a manoeuvrable boom operated by a crew member lying prone at the rear of the fuselage. The receiver flies to a position defined by markings on the underside of the aeroplane and then maintains that station. The boom operator, known as a 'boomer', then adjusts the position of the boom and extends its length so as to engage with a receptacle on the spine of the receiving aircraft.

However, there is a way for the USAF system to be modified so as to allow UK fighters to take fuel using their probes. A 10ft-long hose with a

A Lightning T Mk5 taking fuel from a KC135; note the 90-degree angle between the basket and the hose.

A Lightning F Mk6 with overwing, ferry tanks fills up with American fuel.

USAF Boeing KC135 with a Lightning in tow.

metal drogue/basket can be attached to the end of the boom. The reason for such a short hose is because without any airflow (i.e. while on the ground), it dangles vertically and on take-off the drogue would make contact with the runway. Once in the air, the hose streams horizontally behind the boom and, as long as the boomer keeps everything steady, the RAF aircraft makes contact just as with a normal probe and drogue system. However, that is where the similarity ends. With the UK system the hose must be pushed forward about 10ft to rotate the hose drum and open the valve, allowing fuel to flow. With the USAF modification to their boom system, the receiver must manoeuvre to put a 90-degree angle between the hose and the drogue to open the valve, resulting in an S shape to the hose. Once fuel is flowing, and to ensure that the flow continues, the pilot is, effectively, flying the probe end within a very small pocket of airspace, about 1ft cubed. Moving out of that position causes either the flow to stop or the probe end to break off. This is in contrast to the pilot's familiar UK system where he is free to move 10–15ft forward and back as well as 5-6ft laterally. There was considerable strain put on the weak joint between the probe and the nozzle during cross-nation exercises. As a result, some probe ends broke off, either during the KC135 contacts, or during the weeks following.

With the boom in its stowed position, a Lightning F Mk6 gets up close and personal.

The short hose attached to the boom of a KC135.

Sometimes mishaps occurred. Through no fault of his own this 19 Squadron pilot had the hose from a Victor detach from the hose drum unit and fall to the North German plain.

This Vulcan, XH558, would later have its refuelling modification removed and become the subject of the 'Vulcan to the Skies' project, before finally being grounded in 2015.

Deploying fast jets using tanker support was called a trail. RAF squadrons were required to demonstrate their ability to deploy aircraft, personnel and equipment once a year. For air-defence squadrons, this was achieved by deploying to the Mediterranean for Armament Practice Camp (APC) each year. The Germany Lightning squadrons did their live firing from the NATO base at Decimomannu on the southern tip of Sardinia. In the early 1970s, the UK squadrons detached to RAF Luqa on the island of Malta, but from 1978 on, APCs were held farther east at RAF Akrotiri in Cyprus. Depending on the type of fast jet involved, several tankers would be used. For trails to Cyprus, the tankers established a detachment at Palermo on the island of Sicily and, after giving the fighters a final top-

up to the east of that island, would land there to be ready for their next recipients. There were also trails across the Atlantic for squadrons carrying out ultra-low flying from Goose Bay in Canada or attending the Red and Green Flag exercises at Nellis Air Force Base near Las Vegas.

During the Falklands conflict, a large number of the RAF's Victor tanker fleet was deployed to Ascension Island. This left a gap in the tanker support available to units remaining in the UK. As a stopgap measure, some Vulcan bombers were converted to tankers with an extra tank in the bomb bay and a hose drum unit fitted at the rear of the fuselage. Even though it was a single point supplier, it proved to be a very stable platform from which to take fuel and was popular with the receivers.

The flight engineer's panel on a Tristar showing the CCTV screen so that the refuelling can be monitored. The Victors had a periscope.

The RAF's tanker aircraft evolved over the two decades. The Victor and Vulcan tankers were bombers modified with extra tanks in the bomb bay and had hose drum units fitted. The first, ex-airline, VC10 tankers converted for the RAF had large fuel tanks fitted in what had been the passenger cabin and so were unable to carry many ground crew as passengers. Some of the original RAF VC10 transports, which had been converted into tankers, and the Lockheed Tristars used a different arrangement. The former baggage holds were converted into extra fuel tanks; this left the main deck still available to carry personnel or freight. Such a configuration allowed a Tristar tanker to take four fighters, 100 ground crew and a few tons of equipment quite a considerable distance.

ABOVE AND OPPOSITE: Buccaneer 'buddy buddy' refuelling.

In addition to the large, dedicated tanker aeroplanes, from the Royal Navy the RAF had inherited the capability to use Buccaneer aircraft as tankers. A small hose drum unit, known as a 'buddy pack', was mounted under the wing of the tanker Buccaneer and an extra fuel tank, carrying 2,000 litres, was fitted in the bomb bay. Such an aeroplane was used during a very unusual mission in 1983. In 1982, during the Falklands conflict, RAF Vulcans had carried out bombing missions on the airfield at Stanley, some 3,400nm from their base on Ascension Island, utilizing tanker support. The Vulcans were being replaced by the Tornado GR1, and a question was raised in parliament as to whether a Tornado could carry out a similar mission. IX Squadron, the first Tornado squadron, based at Honington in Suffolk, was tasked with proving it could. The representative target was the airfield at RAF Akrotiri in Cyprus, some 2,250nm from IX Squadron's base. The attacking aircraft would

depart from Honington and meet up with a tanker, which would take the Tornado across France and down into the Mediterranean. The second part of the journey was eastward across Sicily and then south of Crete. The Tornado would then descend to low level, take on fuel from a Buccaneer, and complete the attack run with an airfield attack at Akrotiri before returning to Honington, again with tanker support. The entire sortie would take about 12 hours and several training trips to prove the aircraft's systems (oxygen and engine oil specifically) were carried out by circumnavigating the British Isles twice. On the day, the sortie went without a hitch and was deemed a great success; Britain's politicians were satisfied. However, the attacking Tornado carried four external tanks (therefore, no weapons), and the Buccaneer had taken off from Akrotiri (the target airfield), returning there after having refuelled the Tornado.

A Nimrod MR2 extends its loiter time by taking fuel from a VC10.

One Victor fills to full before taking fast jets somewhere.

F4 Phantoms at dusk with a VC10 tanker.

A 5 Squadron Lightning F Mk6 over the coast of Malta.

A 23 Squadron Tornado F3 overflies Akrotiri airfield in Cyprus.

OPPOSITE: 11 Squadron followed 5 Squadron for an APC in Cyprus and made their mark on this 5 Squadron T Mk5.

Tornado GR1s of 9 Squadron transit south of Greenland with a Victor tanker whilst recovering from Goose Bay in Canada.

A tornado GR1 takes fuel from a Vulcan tanker.

A VC10 K2 accompanied by a VC10 C1 and a 23 Squadron Tornado F3.

A 216 Squadron Tristar with a 5 Squadron Tornado F3.

CHAPTER 6
THE ROYAL AIR FORCE IN GERMANY

When the allies divided the defeated Germany into occupied zones after the Second World War, the UK had an area to the north of the country. There were originally many aerodromes and dozens of squadrons, but by the early 1970s the RAF presence had been scaled down considerably. The Canberras, Javelins and Hunters had all but disappeared and there were only four fast jet airfields. There were three bases near to the Dutch border and they were known as the Clutch stations. They were Bruggen, Wildenrath and Laarbruch. Farther east, and only 80nm from the IGB, was Gutersloh. In addition, there was an RAF base within the British zone in Berlin. RAF Gatow had been a crucial airfield during the Berlin Airlift and continued to be an active airfield throughout the Cold War. No warplanes were allowed along the Berlin air corridors, nor into RAF Gatow, but transports and communication aircraft were permitted to land there. In addition to some Army Air Corps aircraft, two De Havilland Chipmunk T10s were based at Gatow permanently. These aeroplanes were equipped with cameras and frequently flew around the Berlin air traffic control zone which covered the whole of the city and an area of East Germany. Periodically, strike/attack crews from the Clutch stations would be flown to Berlin in a C130 Hercules. With the doors open and the ramp lowered, the pilots and navigators could view potential targets as the Hercules flew over the East German airfields and other military installations that were within the control zone. As has already been covered with air defence of the IGB, RAF Gutersloh was a Lightning base with Nos 19 and 92 squadrons based there until 1976/7. From then

A 19 Squadron Lightning F Mk2A landing at RAF Gutersloh.

OPPOSITE: 31 Squadron re-equipped with the Tornado GR1 in 1984.

on, Gutersloh was home to RAF Germany's Harrier fleet. The role of air defence was taken over by F4 Phantoms re-equipping both 19 and 92 squadrons, which relocated to RAF Wildenrath. This considerably increased the distance that Battle Flight aircraft were from the border, lessening the chance of intercepting any aircraft crossing the IGB.

The two remaining Clutch aerodromes, Bruggen and Laarbruch, retained the same roles, strike/attack and reconnaissance, throughout the 1970s and 1980s. Bruggen had been a Phantom base with Nos 14, 17, and 31 squadrons located there until their aeroplanes were replaced by the Sepecat Jaguar during the mid-1970s. The Jaguars were, in turn, replaced by the Panavia Tornado GR1 from 1984, with 31 Squadron being the first to re-equip. Laarbruch retained the Buccaneer strike/attack aeroplanes throughout the period. However, No 2 Squadron, the only Phantom unit based there, relinquished its reconnaissance role to the Jaguar in 1976 and the re-equipped again in 1988 with the Tornado GR1A.

As well as the Phantoms maintaining two fully armed aeroplanes on Battle Flight at Wildenrath, the other two bases held aircraft on QRA. The nation's nuclear deterrent had been transferred from the RAF's V-force to the Royal Navy's Polaris submarines in the late 1960s. However, the RAF retained some nuclear weapons and the means to deliver them. These were relatively small, tactical WE 177 bombs. A number of the Buccaneers at Laarbruch, and the strike/attack aeroplanes at Bruggen were utilized on QRA and held a 15-minute readiness, each plane with a single nuclear bomb loaded. The intention was to scramble the aircraft in the event of a surprise attack by Warsaw Pact ground forces. The mission was to halt or, at least delay, any advance by destroying strategic targets with single tactical nuclear weapons accurately delivered. The aircrew were required to study the various preselected targets regularly in a secure facility on base. All was planned in meticulous detail. The route was intended to avoid aircraft on similar missions and known surface-to-air missile (SAM) sites. At periodic intervals, the route on the chart would have a notation 'look left', or 'look right'; this was to avoid being blinded by a scheduled weapon detonation in that area. In addition to the route, the target study package included detailed maps, diagrams and high-quality aerial or satellite photographs. These photographs were not only of the target but also of initial points for the final target attack run and any other points of interest along the route. Examples of the targets were bridges, causeways, docks, railway yards and missile sites.

An inert tactical nuclear weapon, the WE177. This was the weapon loaded onto the QRA aircraft at Bruggen and Laarbruch in Germany.

OPPOSITE: A Hawker Siddley Andover of 115 Squadron, a radar calibration unit, was one of the few military types allowed along the air corridor to Berlin.

A 19 Squadron F4 Phantom based at RAF Wildenrath.

A Jaguar GR1 of 31 Squadron, based at RAF Bruggen.

CHAPTER 7

TRAINING FOR WAR, GROUND ATTACK

The business of a peacetime air force is to train for war. Such training will vary considerably depending on the role of the squadron involved. Since the end of the Second World War, radar technology has improved the detection capability and range of both ground-based and airborne radars. The penetration tactic for aeroplanes on interdiction missions was almost exclusively to fly as low and as fast as possible. This was with the intention of flying below the radar cover and significantly delaying detection. It was hoped that this would allow the attacking aircraft to avoid being fired at by SAMs and delay any confrontation with fighters. In the 1980s, the introduction of the Tornado GR1 allowed such missions to be conducted day or night, whatever the weather. The Tornado was equipped with modern avionics in the form of two excellent radars, a computerised navigation system and a very capable autopilot, which facilitated blind flying at high speed and low level. The ground mapping radar (GMR), provided the navigator with a view of the ground ahead that was almost as good as looking at a topographical chart. The terrain following radar (TFR) looked ahead along the planned track and detected any obstacles with vertical extent. The TFR would then send a signal to the autopilot causing the aircraft to fly up and over the hill or obstruction, before descending back down to the selected height. There were settings available to the crew from 200ft to 1,500ft above ground level (AGL). In the early days there were some problems with the TFR, as it was too sensitive. If there was a large, radar significant complex, such as a railway marshalling yard, or a very

large metal-clad building, along the route, the TFR would interpret such a massive radar return as an obstacle even though there was minimal vertical extent. This caused many false climbs and, during hostilities, would have increased the vulnerability of the attackers. A simple solution was found that involved reducing the sensitivity of the TFR by 90%. After that modification, the aeroplane only responded to hazards with true vertical extent.

OPPOSITE: A 31 Squadron Tornado GR1 over the German countryside near the Dutch border.

A Tornado GR1 off the coast of Scotland about to enter the area provided for all-weather, TFR flight.

A 12 Squadron Buccaneer S2 flies low over Möhnesee.

A 20 Squadron Tornado GR1 at low level over Germany.

Tornado GR1s flying in 'goose' formation over the wastes of Canada. This formation allows a swift transition to line astern if bad weather is encountered and TFR flight becomes necessary.

Low-flying fast jets can be very unpopular with the general public, and so there were comprehensive rules and restrictions covering training. Most of the UK's rural areas had a blanket height restriction of 250ft AGL. There were some rather more remote areas of the country where low flying was permitted down to 100ft AGL. In Germany, the blanket restriction was 500ft AGL with designated areas for flight at 250ft AGL. Striving for ever more realistic training, strike/attack units would deploy across the Atlantic to Newfoundland and Nevada. The Canadian air force base at Goose Bay hosted RAF squadrons wishing to practice ultra-low-level flying. There were very few settlements or

The author leading a pair of Tornado GR1s to the Green Flag range in the Nevada desert. 31 Squadron had replaced 617 squadron at Nellis Air Force Base, hence the gold star at the top of the fin on a 617 aeroplane.

inhabitants in the countryside surrounding that part of Canada. In fact, it was possible to fly a two-hour low-level sortie and not see another living thing apart from trees. In the USA, at Nellis Air Force Base near Las Vegas in Nevada, there was a very special training establishment. Large areas of the Nevada desert to the north of Las Vegas were given over to air-to-ground ranges. This was another area where ultra-low-level flying was permitted. The exercises held in this environment were Red Flag and Green Flag. Red Flag was predominantly tactical with the capability of defending fighters and weapon delivery accuracy of the attackers assessed, whereas Green Flag was slanted heavily towards

The view through the head-up display (HUD) of a Tornado GR1. The target is being marked with radar by the navigator. The pilot flies the 'bomb fall line' through the mark and the weapon(s) release when the short crossbar coincides with the mark. Thus, the weapon can be released with great accuracy whilst flying blind.

A visual attack seen through the HUD. The pilot is marking the target (a radar head) visually and flies the 'bomb fall line' through the target rather than through the mark.

electronic warfare tactics. The exercises used some very realistic targets, as well as threats, that could be expected during a conflict in Central Europe. The US military had acquired genuine Soviet bloc radars and other equipment. There were whole airfields laid out in the desert with real aeroplanes scattered around as targets and bombs up to 1,000lb could be dropped. The airfields would be defended by actual Russian

SAM and anti-aircraft artillery (AAA) radars. The training afforded was as authentic as it was possible to be. The ranges were fitted with air combat manoeuvring instrumentation (ACMI), and all participants in these flag exercises carried a transponding pod on an external weapon station. The pods continuously transmitted data about the position, height and energy status of the aircraft and provided all the information required for a thorough debrief after each sortie.

A 27 Squadron Tornado GR1 with an unusual configuration of three 1,500-litre tanks and four 1,000lb inert bombs.

Strike/attack squadrons were able to drop practice weapons on almost every sortie. There were two training weapons available. The 3kg bomb was representative of a cluster bomb, or a retarded 1,000lb bomb. The 28lb training round was used to practice loft, or toss manoeuvres, and simulated a slick 1,000lb bomb, or the tactical nuclear weapons that were loaded onto the aircraft holding QRA in Germany. Both of these training bombs and the weapons that they represented were unguided 'dumb' bombs. They were carried in a streamlined body called a carrier bomb light stores (CBLS). It was about the same size as a 1,000lb bomb but carried four training bombs and each could be released separately. Following the introduction of the Tornado GR1, with its sophisticated navigation and weapon-aiming systems, the accuracy achieved when delivering these dumb weapons was quite impressive. Throughout the UK and Western Europe there were a considerable number of live-bombing and gunnery ranges where crews could test their skills at weapon delivery. In the UK, most of the ranges were along the east coast, with others in Wales and Scotland. The most realistic training was afforded by entering the ranges on a first run attack (FRA) basis. A training sortie would be planned so that at some stage the route passed close to one of the available ranges. A time slot would be booked before take-off and a required time on target (TOT) allocated to each of the crews in a formation. When a number of aircraft attack the same target with laydown weapons, which require overflight of the target, there must be a delay so that the previous attacker's bomb does not destroy the next. For retarded 1,000lb bombs, the interval between attacking aeroplanes should be a minimum of 25 seconds. Of course, once the first bombs are dropped, defending forces would be on high alert and so each crew would have a different attack track to fly. However, on a training

range safety considerations require that the same attack track is used for each weapon delivery. For this reason, the formation would split some distance from the range to achieve different tracks to the initial point (IP), thereby practising the technique required during hostilities whilst observing the peacetime safety requirements of dropping training bombs. Some of the ranges also offered targets for the practice of air-to-ground gunnery. Apart from the Buccaneer, all of the RAF's strike/attack aircraft were equipped with guns. The Harrier and Jaguar were fitted with Aden 30mm cannons. Each round from an Aden cannon weighed about 1kg and, if they were high explosive (HE) rounds, each was the equivalent of

OPPOSITE: A 20 Squadron GR1 at low level showing two CBLS carried on each under fuselage pylon. The carrier is empty, so they've already been to the range.

Practice weapons for a Tornado GR1. A CBLS with a 3kg (6.6lb) practice retard bomb on the left and a 28lb practice loft weapon on the right. To rear of the CBLS is an inert 1,000lb bomb.

Direct hit. The releasing aircraft can be seen at bottom left, giving an idea of the separation from the explosion.

A lofted bomb narrowly misses the target. It would have been close enough for a nuclear weapon but unsatisfactory for a high-explosive one.

a hand grenade delivered to target at supersonic speed, with devastating results. The F4 Phantom had no internal gun but could be fitted with a Vulcan 20mm gun pod on the centre, under fuselage, pylon. This gun operated on the Gatling gun principle with rotating barrels, and so achieved a rate of fire in the region of 6,000 rounds per minute, or 100 per second. The Tornado sported a Mauser 27mm cannon, which was very similar to the Aden cannon previously used extensively in the RAF.

These training sorties and training rounds provided the opportunity to practise missions and delivery tactics on a daily basis at relatively low cost. However, simulation never quite matches the real experience. During each tour of duty every crew would be allocated a number of

real weapons to deliver, (nuclear bombs being the exception, of course). Several ranges in the UK and Germany permitted the dropping of inert 1,000lb bombs, but there was one range off the north coast of Scotland were crews could practice with live 1,000lb bombs. Garvie Island lies almost a mile from the coast, near Cape Wrath. It is roughly the size and shape of a naval destroyer and provides an ideal target for high-explosive ordnance, having both horizontal and vertical extent. A laydown attack entails overflight of the target, having dropped a retarded weapon or weapons. The retardation ensures that the bomb explodes some time after the delivery aircraft has overflown the target, not vertically below it as a slick weapon would. A loft delivery allows

TORNADO - OFFSET LOFT

The principle for offset loft, attacking a target that cannot be seen visually or on radar.

A bomb fitted with laser guidance equipment that virtually guaranteed a direct hit every time.

for the bomb to be delivered without overflight of the target and is particularly suitable for heavily defended targets. The attacking aeroplane runs in on the attack track at low level and high speed. Utilizing a prominent feature, which may be visually identifiable or radar significant, the required pull-up point can be calculated. At the appropriate time the aircraft enters a 3G pull into a 45-degree climb. The weapon is released some five miles from target, allowing the delivering attack aircraft to reverse course and dive back to low level in an escape manoeuvre. This delivery method is also suitable for delivering tactical nuclear bombs. As technology advanced, so did weapon accuracy; it was usual to be able to deliver a weapon using the

loft manoeuvre to within 100ft of the target. Accuracy with a laydown attack was around 20ft. With the introduction of laser range finding, the accuracy improved still further. In 1985, a formation of four Tornado GR1s of 31 Squadron flew a sortie which included a range detail in northern Germany. The target was an obsolete tank and each Tornado carried four 3kg training bombs in a CBLS. All 16 bombs were dropped from 200ft and 540 knots during laydown attacks, utilizing laser range finding. There were 14 direct hits and the other two bombs landed within 10ft of the target. This was impressive for dumb bombs. Of course, in the years to follow the introduction of laser guided bombs (LGB) would virtually guarantee a direct hit for every delivery.

A GR1 releases a live 1,000lb retard bomb on the range at Garvie Island.

The author dropping four 1,000lb retard bombs at Tain range in Scotland.
(Photo courtesy of BAE SYSTEMS)

A pair of 31 Squadron GR1s en route to the north of Scotland to drop live 1,000lb bombs on the range at Garvie Island.

OPPOSITE: A Phantom of 228 OCU with a Vulcan 20mm cannon mounted on the centreline and two training Skyflash rounds on the forward, recessed stations.

CHAPTER 8

TRAINING FOR WAR, AIR DEFENCE

Decisions made by various governments in the 1950s and 1960s almost saw the demise of the Royal Air Force in its familiar form of the 1970s and 1980s. It was considered that the manned fighter was becoming obsolete and should be replaced by SAMs, just as the manned bomber should be replaced by ballistic missiles. As a consequence of such deliberations, research and development of new military aeroplanes all but stopped in the UK. Fortunately, the Lightning had entered service in 1961 and a series of developments of that magnificent fighter ensured that it remained on the front line of UK air defence until the late 1980s. However, a lingering desire to rely on missiles was to have a significant effect on the armament of Britain's fighters. The early marks of the Lightning were armed with two Firestreak infrared, heat-seeking missiles and two Aden 30mm cannon. There was an option to replace the missiles with 48 two-inch, unguided rockets intended to be fired at a formation of bombers. However, this concept was quite short lived. A major development of the Lightning was the F Mk3 with more powerful engines, an improved radar, and Red Top infrared missiles. However, the Aden 30mm cannons had been removed. The Red Top missiles did have a head-on capability, whereas the Firestreaks were strictly stern-attack only weapons. The Lightning was always limited by a small fuel load and two developments corrected that deficiency. The F Mk2A and the F Mk6 versions had a large integral fuel tank that increased the fuel capacity by almost 50 per cent. Being an updated version of an earlier mark of the aircraft, the F Mk2A retained the two Aden cannons. The F Mk6, however, had no guns but an option

was developed to replace the forward part of the ventral fuel tank with a gun pack housing two Adens. This was later to become the standard configuration for the Lightning F Mk6. The F4 Phantoms bought for the Royal Navy and the RAF did not have an integral gun fitted. They had

The author with 'his' Lightning F Mk2A. The position of the upper gun ports is shown clearly (the Aden cannons are mounted behind the cockpit) as is the Firestreak missile. Also of note is the blanking plate covering the lower gun port (the missile pack could be swapped for two more Aden cannons).

OPPOSITE: 5 Squadron swapped its Lightnings for the Tornado F3 in 1988.

ABOVE AND ABOVE RIGHT: A Lightning F Mk2A showing a ventral tank entirely for fuel.

A more modern Lightning F Mk3 with no guns fitted.

to load an external 20mm gun pod (a Vulcan six-barrelled Gatling-type gun firing 6,000 rounds per minute), on a centreline station under the fuselage. When the air defence variant of the Tornado (F3) finally entered service in the late 1980s, it only had one integral gun, whereas the GR1 had two. This was because the space in the forward fuselage was needed to house the retractable refuelling probe, which was a permanent feature on the left side of the aeroplane. On the Tornado GR1 the probe was externally fitted on the right-hand side, and removable, although it later remained attached almost all the time.

Normal day-to-day air-defence training involved practice intercepts (PI), air combat manoeuvring (ACM) and low-level affiliation. PIs could vary from low level (250ft) right up to high level (55,000ft+), and the fighters could receive control from ground control intercept (GCI) radar stations or airborne radar platforms such as the Shackleton AEW, or Boeing E3A AWACS aircraft. The targets could be similar aircraft types

ABOVE AND ABOVE RIGHT: Standard fit for the F Mk6 was to have the forward part of the ventral tank replaced by a gun pack housing two Aden cannons.

as fighters would usually fly PI training in pairs and take turns as the target. In addition, external assets would provide targets, such as 360 Squadron's Canberra T17s, which offered electronic warfare training by jamming the fighter's radar or interfering with the control instructions being given by GCI. Vulcans would often act as targets at high level and gave experience of infrared decoy tactics. When filing a flight plan, any aircraft had the option to add the word 'embellish' in the remarks section. That action would send a comment to the air defence system that the flight was available as a target for UK air defence forces. This was very useful training and similar to a QRA scenario. The intercept was offered to fighters that were already airborne but didn't have to be

accepted. The value was in the variety of targets that might be presented. They could be training aircraft or transports at low, medium, or high levels. Infrequently, they could even be a helicopter. In August 1979, the MoD chartered a very special aircraft as a target for exercise *Alvernia*. The aircraft was a British Airways Concorde and it was tasked to fly two racetracks that extended for approximately 350 miles of the North Sea. Fighters from all of the air defence bases in the UK were allocated times to attack this Mach 2.2, 55,000ft target heading south from abeam Scotland. Only head-on attacks were permitted and, following a simulated missile launch at Mach 1.5, the fighter just flew straight ahead, decelerating to subsonic speed and returned to base. A closing speed

Tornado GR1s of 15 Squadron.

well in excess of Mach 3 is almost 40 miles per minute and was hitherto virtually unseen on RAF interceptors' radars. The only comparable target was France's Mirage IV bomber.

ACM training was mostly between similar types, but it was important to carry out a significant amount of dissimilar air combat training (DACT). As a result of the experience gained by US forces during the Vietnam War, it was realised that close manoeuvring between fighters, or dog fighting, was an important skill to train to achieve. The official policy of relying entirely on air-to-air missiles was shown to be flawed as well. Although, as the capability of the various missiles improved, the edge certainly went to the missile. The requirement to visually identify an opponent as hostile was also a factor in determining tactics. The US Navy set up its fighter weapons school, more commonly known as Top Gun, to teach the art of ACM. The USAF had a slightly different approach and created aggressor squadrons. These units flew small, agile fighters with faux Soviet markings, and the instructor pilots were trained

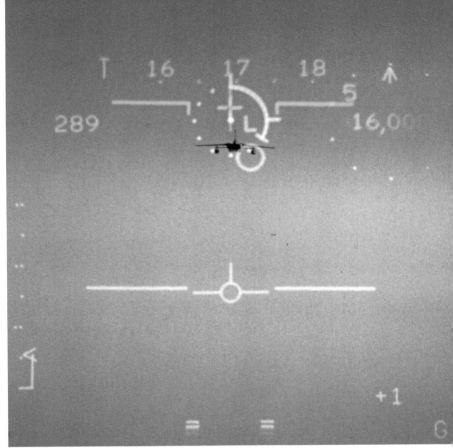

The view through the HUD of a Tornado F3. The radar is locked onto the starboard drop tank of the target and the range is 400 yards. The short bar indicates the ideal range to fire (300 yards) but the pipper (centre of the circle) needs to be moved onto the target.

OPPOSITE: A XIX Squadron Phantom with a full load of eight missiles and a Vulcan 20mm cannon.

to fly them using Soviet tactics, replicating the capabilities of various Russian fighters. The USAF's aggressor squadrons were based in various parts of the world, but one was based at RAF Alconbury in Cambridgeshire. The training was available to all the European NATO air forces and the RAF took full advantage of the opportunity. DACT was an integral part of every fast jet squadron's training and all of the RAF's combat aircraft were involved, either with other UK assets or their NATO allies.

Low-level affiliation was valuable training for both the attacking and defending aeroplanes. A strike/attack formation would contact an air-defence squadron and give an approximate location, generally overland, and a time window for transit of the area. The fighters would set up a CAP and wait for the trade to appear. The subsequent engagement might be simulating the use of air-to-air missiles, or even the use of guns if the required parameters for missile launch could not be met. In the 1970s, the North German plain was a target-rich environment with a large number of aircraft from the various NATO nations using the area for low-level training. The Lightning squadrons at Gutersloh set up a special telephone request service which was called Dial a Lightning and provided fighters to intercept the low-flying aeroplanes and deliver effective affiliation training.

The effectiveness of the various types of air-defence training was assessed by the use of film. Every fighter carried at least

84 Squadron at Akrotiri was equipped with the Wessex 5 from the mid-1980s. The squadron provided a search-and-rescue service and support to the UN peace keeping forces on Cyprus.

The banner used for practicing air-to-air gunnery. It is 30ft long by 6ft high. However, when approaching from the rear preparing to fire, it only appears to be about 6ft by 8ft.

A Tornado F3 closes in on the banner for a firing pass. The towing Canberra is in a turn to minimise the chance of being hit by stray rounds and give the fighter a chance of stabilizing its approach.

A banner being inspected by senior officers in Malta. Up to four different aircraft can fire on one banner. Each firing aeroplane is loaded with rounds that have been dipped in paint to leave a mark as they pass through the target.

one camera that supplied images of the target, and they could be used to decide whether a claimed kill was valid or not. In addition, recordings were made of the radar information so that not only the veracity of the kill could be assessed but also the effectiveness of the intercept. Because the opposition was always a manned aircraft during this air-defence training, actual weapons could not be fired in the way that training bombs were dropped by the strike/attack forces. It was necessary to prove the accuracy and effectiveness of the weapons carried by the fighters and interceptors of the RAF. Therefore, each squadron sent aircraft and crews to two annual events. As previously mentioned, each air defence unit was required to demonstrate their capability to deploy the whole squadron. This was achieved by detaching from the UK for an annual armament practice camp (APC). These camps were used to hone the pilots' skill in air-to-air gunnery against a towed target and give the ground crews experience in arming, then re-arming the aeroplanes. The target was a hessian banner, which was about 30ft long and 6ft wide. Inert rounds, which had been dipped in coloured paint, were fired. If the towed banner were hit the bullet would leave a coloured smudge as it passed through. Up to four fighters would fire at the banner during a single sortie. They each fired rounds that had been dipped in different coloured paint, and so it was possible to ascertain who had hit the target and with what success. The other annual event did not involve the whole squadron but a small detachment of five or six aircraft with a similar number of crews. Missile practice camp (MPC) was a means of giving crews the experience of firing an air-to-air missile and also assessing the effectiveness of the weapon. Air-to-air missiles are expensive items of hardware and so each crew was limited to firing only one during a tour of duty (generally around three years). The range where most missiles were fired was in Cardigan Bay on the west coast of Wales, and the detachment was to RAF Valley on the island of Anglesey. Both semi-active radar and infrared heat-seeking missiles were fired at targets towed by an unmanned aircraft, or a drone. The tugs were operated from a facility at RAF Llanbedr and the whole operation was controlled from a radar station at Aberporth. In addition to the annual MPC, QRA aircraft would

periodically be scrambled to transit over to Wales and fire a missile. This was to validate the whole process from reaction time through the transit, concluding in a successful intercept with the eventual accomplishment of a destroyed target.

A Tornado F3 fires an AIM 9L Sidewinder missile on the range in Cardigan Bay.

OPPOSITE: This Tornado GR1 has the detachable refuelling probe clearly visible below the cockpit canopy.

XI and 23 Squadron Tornado F3s from RAF
Leeming in North Yorkshire

A Tornado F3 of 23 Squadron showing the full complement of weaponry.

A 5 Squadron F3 in the 67 wing position.

OPPOSITE: Vertical flight by F3s of 23 and 5 squadrons, both showing off a full weapon load.

Wing tip vortices from Tornado F3s in a tight turn.

OPPOSITE: A Canberra T17 of 360 Squadron, which supplied electronic warfare training to all of the UK's armed forces.

A Harrier GR5.

OPPOSITE: Canberras of 100 Squadron provided target towing facilities for air-to-air firing.

A Canberra tug. The line towing the banner target can be seen
streaming from the belly of the aeroplane.

A Meteor F Mk8 converted into a drone to tow targets for practice air-to-air missile firing, when the infrared target source would be towed 700ft behind the tug. In this photograph the cockpit is empty, but the aircraft can be flown conventionally with a pilot on board.

CHAPTER 9
INTERACTION WITH NATO ALLIES

Each year, a programme of NATO squadron exchanges was arranged. RAF fast jet squadrons would take a small contingent of aircraft, crews and ground crew to an airbase of another nation. A similarly sized detachment from that base would proceed in the other direction and be hosted by those remaining on the squadron. Such exchanges usually lasted ten days and were an opportunity for interaction between allies. There would be a considerable amount of flying and, as the exchanging squadrons were generally from different roles, different tactics could be observed and countered. There was, of course, plenty of time for socializing as well and many enduring friendships and affiliations were created.

The multinational Flag exercises in the USA have already been mentioned and the concept lead to a similar arrangement in Europe. In 1978, ten NATO members formed the Tactical Leadership Programme (TLP) as a series of theoretical seminars held over a two-week period. The venue was the German air force base of Furstenfelbruck, near Munich, and aircrew from the different NATO members were invited to attend and discuss tactics and procedures. In 1979, the course was extended by two weeks to include a flying phase. At the same time, the location was moved to the Luftwaffe airfield at Jever in Northern Germany, where it remained until the end of 1988. The flying phase was organized so that a strike/attack package would be given a route and targets to attack. The air

defence, or counter air, participants would be given limited information about that route but enough to ensure that at least one engagement would occur. The planning, execution and debriefing of each sortie took all day, but the lessons learned were most valuable. After graduation from TLP, the participants would return to their units and spread the word. TLP was, and still is, considered a centre of excellence and the qualification is well regarded by all fast jet aircrew throughout NATO.

RIGHT: Tornado F3s of 11 and 23 squadrons from RAF Leeming.

OPPOSITE: A NATO squadron exchange between XI Squadron at Binbrook and Luftwaffe Lockheed F104 Starfighters from Jever.

Another squadron exchange between 23 Squadron Tornados and French Mirage 2000s.

Eskisehir in Turkey was the venue for this exchange between 5 Squadron and Turkish F4s in 1988.

CHAPTER 10
DEFROST, IT'S ALL OVER

In the late 1980s, there were a series of nuclear weapons treaties between the USA and the USSR, and significant internal reforms were made by the Soviet leader, Gorbachev. In 1987, the US President, Ronald Reagan, famously challenged him to tear down the Berlin Wall in a speech made at the Brandenburg Gate. The wall came down in November 1989. There were revolutions throughout communist Europe that year, which led to the collapse of the Warsaw Pact and the gradual withdrawal of Soviet forces. Finally, at the end of 1991, the USSR was dissolved, separating into 15 independent nations. The Cold War was most definitely over!

LEFT AND ABOVE: In September 1988, two Russian MiG 29 Fulcrums visited the Farnborough air show. The first Russian fighters to land in the UK since the end of WWII, they were intercepted by Tornado F3s of 5 Squadron.

OPPOSITE: A Tornado F3 closes in to echelon port on the author's aircraft.

5 Squadron put up a formation of Tornado F3s.

A Lightning heads home at midnight in the summer.

A VC10 tanker and a Nimrod MR2 over the Moray Firth.